GW01465221

'ies

Boobs & Bums

by Charlie Watson

Illustrations by Richard Lowdell

Nightingale

An imprint of Wimbledon Publishing Company
LONDON

Copyright © 2000
Illustrations © 2000 WPC

First published in Great Britain in 2000
by Wimbledon Publishing Company Ltd
P.O. Box 9779 London SW19 7ZG
All rights reserved

First published 2000 in Great Britain

ISBN: 1903222 10 9

Produced in Great Britain
Printed and bound in Hungary

Boobs

and Bums

This book has been crafted with a sense of wonder and awe at the many variations of the human anatomy which separate and differentiate human beings. More specifically, it acknowledges that the Creator of these variations must have a splendid sense of humour. Whilst evolution has not toyed too much with mundane things like arms and legs, eyes, ears or fingers, it seems there has been little respite for the 'rude bits'. And if some of us wobble whilst others droop, and some of us totter whilst others stoop, it's usually because Him upstairs has decided to hand ridiculous and strange ornaments on our private areas.

The question we must ask ourselves is, what do we want to do about this? Starve, fast or sculpt ourselves until our bodies look the way we want them to? Or accept the divine joke and understand that this is one of the many ways we have all been made individuals? This book of poetry is written to help everyone 'get the joke'. Most of us are in here somewhere. Some of us might even be in it twice...Lucky devils.

Charlie Watson
1999

The Large Breast

They started to flower when I was a child
A blossoming swell in my breast,
So off I went down to the lingerie store
And asked them to measure my chest.
By ten I had tripled the size of my cup
By twelve I supported two kegs,
And now I believe it's been 25 years
Since last I had sight of my legs.

The Drooping Nipple

They say I've got perfect proportions
Indeed my statistics are fine,
But some of my hidden distinctions
Are fruits of a shoddy design.
My boyfriends have yearned for me fiercely
Their passions, however, abate,
Confronted with tits like a clock face
And nipples at twenty past eight.

Unlikely Twins

The boob on my right takes a D cup
The boob on my left takes a B,
My right bosom weighs in at 500 grams
My left one at 73.
One boob points up, the other points down
But many like these can be found,
The one major feature that sets mine apart
Is one boob is square and one's round.

The Banana Breast

Until God gave me bosoms
I thought that they'd be round,
But mine grew long and slender
And curled up from the ground.
Still, there's fun at bath-time -
My hubbie's found the knack,
Of hanging undies on my hooks
To make a clothing rack.

The Large Nipple

The women in Playboy perplex me
Their nipples like pert little grapes,
A genuine woman's got genuine nipples
Take mine, which are like dinner plates.

The Pert Bust

Like freshly-set jelly -
My boobies are firm,
And gravity can't pull them down.
My boobies point skyward
On two perfect puddings,
That seem to fear facing the ground.

The Natural Sag

I don't much care for silicon
It's not the natural way,
My body's prone to sagginess
So that's the way I'll stay.
All that Baywatch beauties have
A Wonderbra achieves,
And when I'm old and need a laugh
They'll swing between my knees.

The Builder's Bum

It's not by fluke of fortune
My botty cleavage shows,
There's neither belt nor trouser
That can my cheeks enclose.
And since a major part of work
Is leering at the totty,
It's nice to turn around and show
A firm, seductive botty.

The Small Breast

In showers after P.E. class
I used to feel so glum,
My friends were sporting giant boobs
Compared to my two plums.
But now with age my views have changed
'Coz still my plums look bold,
And all my friends have monstrous jugs
No scaffold can uphold.

The Hairy Bum

If vanity were more my thing
I'd boost our chemist's funds,
And buy a thousand razor blades
To shave between my buns.
But after several day's of silk
The forest would fight back,
And I'd rather have a hairy bum
Than stubble in my crack

The Prosperous Bum

I notice that people admire
The cushions of meat on my bum,
The contours that make me a lady
And furnish a seat for my son.
My buttocks are signs that I'm wealthy
Their prominence shows I'm well-fed,
And no one has ever objected
For fear that I'd sit on their head.

The Tight Bum

When it comes to muscular buns
I know that I have a fine set.
The price that I pay?
Just four hours a day
On a Stair Master covered in sweat.

The Plentiful Cleavage

The valley between the two bosoms
Is useful when out with a guy,
It has several functions on offer
Provided it catches his eye.
It's handy for keeping him randy
Or simply to keep his hands warm,
And snuggling up at the movies
It makes a great tub for popcorn.

The Pear-shaped Rear

My chest is magnificent, slim is my waist
However, my hips are quite girthy,
Framing a bottom that gives me the ballast
To keep me well-grounded and earthy.
Waist up, I'm a model with slender physique
Waist down, I balloon like a whale,
But if I'm knocked down I come rolling back up
And can walk undeterred in a gale.

The Suctioned Bum

I've photos to prove that I used to be fat
Despite all my jogging and fasting.
I read Eastern wisdom and watched Rikki Lake
But my botty flab seemed everlasting.
One day as I sat with my half bowl of fruit
I realised these methods lacked clout,
So went to the surgeon, revealed my cheeks
And ordered he hoover them out.

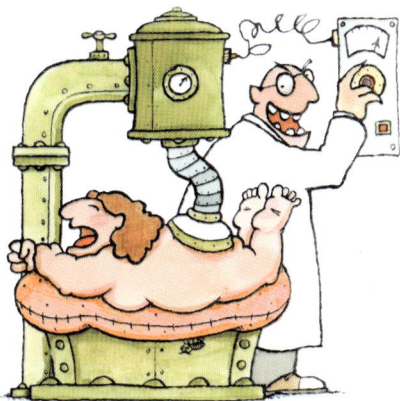

The Fake Breast

I owe my fine titties to Heinrich
The man who made boobies his art,
He sculpted my peaches to melons
And thus the doc captured my heart.
Our honey-moon several months later
Was planned for his Spanish abode,
But as our plane climbed to its zenith
Thin air caused my breasts to explode.

The Cellulite Bum

It's funny that when you grow big
Your skin doesn't stretch very tight,
But gathers in dimples and dents
That science has called 'cellulite.'
Our girlish illusions of beauty
Are shattered as youthfulness leaves,
The day we discover our buttocks
Have turned into fresh cottage cheese.

The Spotty Botty

I'm blessed with the spottiest bottom
The medical world's ever seen,
My doctor said my pimpled behind
Is a dermatological dream.
Being so timid it took me some years
To finally make a bloke mine,
Only to find out he'd made me his muse
For a thesis on pizza design.

The Cute Bum

It's fun to bend over and give men a thrill
My bum is like sex on a stick,
And sometimes I don't like to stand up at all
As my face tends to make people sick.

Flabby Tits

If I lived in Tokyo
I'd be a sumo star
But no - I'm just
A bloke from Stoke
Who needs to wear a bra.

The Flat Bum

My insubstantial buttocks
Barely stick out from my back,
And so I have no bum per se
Just long legs then a crack.
Yet though perhaps unshapely
An up-side I have found:
I have the perfect frame to wear
My knickers both ways round.

Nipple Whiskers

Some people think it natural
Some people think it weird,
That if I leave my breasts uncropped
My nipples sprout a beard.
Now body hair is part of being
Human, this I know,
But must I have the sort of breasts
Orang-utans might grow?

Untanned Breasts

I don't like people staring
At my boobies on the beach,
I wrap a towel around me
To ensure they're out of reach.
Whilst others tan, the towel protects
The chest and upper legs,
My face becoming golden
While my breasts look like fried eggs.

The Long Nipple

If God is a practical joker
Then surely I suffer his best,
Look! In the place of a nipple
A thumb on the end of my breast!

Cut~out Nipples

Cut out and glue to your nipples for fun and frolics

SUPASTAR

SUPASTAR

WARNING: DO NOT USE SUPER GLUE.

The Inverted Nipple

They're shy I tell my boyfriends
A kiss won't make them pert,
I need a suction pump to make
My nipples extrovert.

Unrequited Dreams

I have a dream from time to time
The clouds are raining breasts
And in my joy I run to each
To sneak a quick caress.
But just as things are heating up
And ecstasy seems near,
The dream becomes a nightmare
And I wake up, stiff with fear.

The Third Nipple

I want to pretend that it's only a wart
Yet know this is how I was born:
To suffer the gibes that I might be a witch,
A demon or Lucifer's spawn.
I went to the doctor's and told him my fears
He said, 'Madam, please take a seat,
You're carrying triplets and 'coz you're a freak
Your babies will each get a teat!'

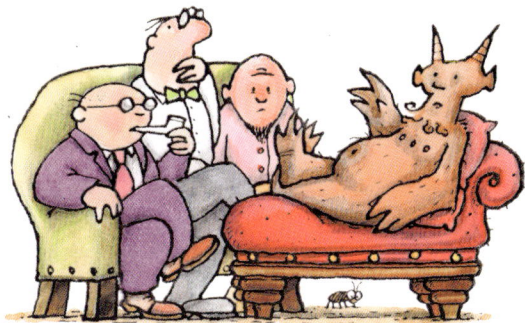

The Bombay Botty

Thanks to my Friday night curry
Today I'll be chained to the loo
Already the bulk of this morning
Was spent passing warm vindaloo.

Bye!